Take Good Care of Me

What Kids Think Every Grown-Up Needs to Know About Being a Parent

Created by Kari Cimbalik

Sourcebooks, Inc.
Naperville, IL

Library of Congress Cataloging-in-Publication
Cimbalik, Kari.
Take good care of me : children tell grownups what they want and need / edited by Kari Cimbalik.
p. cm.
ISBN 1-57071-442-8 (alk. paper)
1. Parenting. 2. Children's writings. 3. Children's drawings. 4. Parent and child. I. Title.
HQ755.8.c488   1999   98-33195
649'.1—dc21   CIP

Published by Sourcebooks, Inc.

P.O. Box 372
Naperville, IL 60566
630-961-3900
Fax: 630-961-2168

ISBN 1-57071-442-8

Printed and bound in the United States of America.
10 9 8 7 6 5 4 3 2 1

To my mother, who taught my sister and me
the important things in life and kept
us a family after the death of our father.

Acknowledgements

I would like to extend my sincere thanks to Mrs. Fouts, principal of Morrish Elementary School in Swartz Creek, Michigan for helping me get this book underway. I would also like to thank the teachers of Morrish Elementary School for allowing me into their classroom and getting the children involved in this project. But, most importantly of all, I would like to thank each and every one of the children who contributed this wonderful artwork and these insightful views on parenting.

I am fortunate for the opportunities during my life to be around kids for they have inspired me more than they will ever know. I am especially grateful for my nieces, Krisha, Alesha, Morgan, and Gabrielle and my nephew, A.J. These little "angels" became my inspiration for this book and have shown me that it is really the simple things in life that matter most.

I am thankful for my Grandmother who encouraged and helped me pursue my dreams no matter what they were. I am also thankful for my sister, Kelly who is more than just my sister; she's my best friend and has always stood by me. I also would like to thank the rest of my family and my friends for their never-ending support in my endeavors and for always believing in me.

I would especially like to thank Shelly Cole for keeping after me to finish this book and keeping me focused on my goals. She was the logical one and kept me moving forward when I became overwhelmed by the tasks along the way. Her faith in me and her never-ending support are gifts I will always cherish.

I am very grateful to Tim Patrick (Tim #1072) for his encouragement and unfailing friendship. He kept me on track to meet my deadlines and coached me along until the book was finalized.

I would like to thank the Writers Rendezvous group of Bloomfield Hills, Michigan. This group of talented writers provided me with constructive criticism to make this a better book and encouraged me to follow through with my ideas.

Throughout my life there have been people too numerous to mention who have touched my world and guided me along the way. To these individuals, and I hope you know who you are, I am forever grateful.

Table of Contents

Love is for Children.

Artwork by Megan, age 9

How Can Your Mother and Father Be Better Parents?

Our parents try to teach us not to smoke and not to talk to strangers. My mom taught me how to be polite. My dad taught me never to fight in school or at home. But they both are the best parents in the world. I love my parents. My mom and dad are always there for me when I need them. It takes a lot of effort to be a parent.

Stacee, age 9

A good parent can talk to you without yelling. And they can understand what you are talking about. A good parent lets you stay up a little bit longer when your favorite show is an extra hour.

Carin, age 11

How they can be better parents is they can do the dishes and my brother Aaron and I can watch TV or something like that.

Amanda, age 9

Artwork by Matt, age 7

I think for a parent to be the best they need to spend a lot of fun time with their kids. Playing with kids makes the parents and the children feel good. I think a parent should not be so crabby at their child unless they get in trouble.

Khyl, age 10

I would tell them to spend more time with me.

Timothy, age 6

Artwork by Gregory, age 8

Lots of love and caring, also being there when your child needs you. Taking good care of your child, giving them food and shelter is what makes a good parent.

Debbie, age 9

I would tell them to give a little allowance and buy healthy food.

Weston, age 10

I would tell my parents to be patient, love me a lot and keep helping me.

Mike, age 10

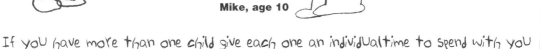

If you have more than one child give each one an individual time to spend with you

Artwork by Allisa, age 9

I want my mom and dad to kiss me every night at bedtime because I love them. I want my mom to teach me how to do the dishes because then she would not have to do them.

Tori, age 6

What makes a good parent is not letting your kids stay up too late watching TV. Also get your kids involved in sports or activities.

Jason, age 9

I would tell them to be good to their children and to set a good example for them.

Cathy, age 8

Artwork by Taylor, age 6

They could be more understanding. They could not yell at you and try to help. They should not do things that we can't do.

Laura, age 9

I would tell them to be fair.

Todd, age 9

Help your children do things right

Love me even if I'm bad

I could help my parents be better parents. Well, here's some tips. Be loving and caring and don't always scream or sometimes they will get scared.

Melissa, age 9

Artwork by Laura, age 9

Listen to the kids and be good to the kids. Love your kids. Be friends with your kids and most of all lock your doors at night so robbers don't get your kids.

Taylor, age 7

I would tell them that you should try to put your feet in their shoes to see how they feel.

Brad, age 10

They could relax more and not work so hard so they could be more patient and spend more time with me.

Mike, age 10

A good parent listens to their kids, teaches them things and helps them all the time.

Mike, age 10

Maybe not yell so much. Show a good example
for me. And when I get in fights ask me what
I should have done to prevent the fight.

Emily, age 8

Be a shining example for me to follow.

I think they could be better parents by not just doing
whatever the child wants or spoiling him/her, but by just
being better at not taking your temper out on them.
Just set them aside and ask them why they did this.

Alissa, age 9

What is the Most Important Thing Your Parents Should Teach You?

They should teach you never to do bad things. That you should never be mean to people. Be nice to people at school and everywhere else. Always be yourself and don't try to act like someone or something just to impress them.

Debbie, age 9

They should teach you right from wrong, safety first and it's alright just try and try again.

Laura, age 9

Having confidence in me that I can do anything I put my mind to. To mind my manners.

Eric, age 7

Artwork by Mike, age 10

They can teach me to be confident, faithful, respectful and always looking out for the little ones.

Kim, age 9

The most important thing is the difference between right and wrong.

Nick, age 8

I think the most important thing your parents should teach you is not to do drugs and get in fights.

Joey, age 10

Artwork by Meghan, age 7

Roots and wings are wonderful things!

I think that the most important thing my parents can teach me is to be myself. I don't have to dress, act or be anybody to be cool. I just have to be myself. I don't want to be anybody else. I just want to act the way I act, dress the way I dress. I am just the person I can be and I have to act confident. You have got to be confident or else you won't feel good about yourself and you won't be cool.

Joshua, age 8

How to live right, what to do if there's an emergency and to be nice.

Deanta, age 10

Thank you

Artwork by Aaron, age 8

To know and love God and respect
all of his creations.

Dominique, age 7

I think the most important thing
my parents can teach me is
manners and self respect.

Adrienne, age 10

The most important thing that your parents can teach you is the facts of life.

Steven, age 9

Don't do drugs-don't sell drugs. To say please and thank you. To say excuse me. To say nice things to people. To say please pass the peas. To say if someone says thank you, be sure to say you're welcome. Not to push by people.

Samira, age 10

I would like to learn from my parents to respect others.

Lauren, age 10

Artwork by Marcus, age 10

The most important thing that your parents can teach you is to be a good person who has good character and is honest, helpful and kind.

Mike, age 10

care

JOB

Education

Love

Appreciation

Believe in yourself!

Respecting other people is the most important thing a parent can teach you.

Emily, age 8

They can teach you manners and sharing.

Todd, age 9

How to be a very good student. How to read. How to do things like math. How to love and respect each other. To stay in school. To be the best person I can be and to like myself. To love my sister and to teach me right from wrong.

Kassi, age 7

reach for the stars of life

Artwork by Michelle, age 10

What Should Parents Know About Kids?

Kids have their own ideas and a lot of good ones. Parents should take the time to listen to their kids. Parents should know that their kids love them. Kids like to be respected just like their parents do. Kids will be kids and parents will be parents. Kids like to have fun and laugh.

Jessica, age 7

I think parents should know what their kid's favorite food is, what kind of clothes their kid likes to wear, and what sports their kids like to play. I also think that parents should know what their kid's favorite color is.

Aaron, age 10

Artwork by Trevor, age 8

Kids like to stay up and watch TV until they get tired. They like to eat food while they watch TV. Us girls don't like to wear dresses to church, on holidays or to school. Instead we like to wear jeans and a sweat shirt. We certainly don't like to eat veggies or drink milk and juices, instead we like to drink pop.

Dawn, age 10

Parents should know that kids don't like to be yelled at.

Katie, age 10

Parents should know that kids like ice cream and most girls don't like dresses. Kids also don't like their parents to buy clothes for them. The parents should know what foods are liked and disliked.

Michelle, age 11

Artwork by Jennifer, age 7

They should know what's going on in their lives. If they're doing good in school or if something is wrong in their lives, if they're taking drugs.

Laura, age 9

Parents should always know what is on the child's mind. If it looks like something is wrong or if their child has a problem, the parent should always take time out and have a talk with the child and express their feelings on how to solve the problem.

Alissa, age 9

Artwork by Sheena, age 10

Parents should know that we like to have our own way, if we don't we will cry.

Mike, age 9

Young brothers or sisters that do not like the older brother or sister often lie to get them in trouble. When you are told not to do something and your parents leave, you do it. When you can't go somewhere, you say that you're going somewhere else and you go where you can't go.

John, age 8

Kids do what their parents do when they are young. Kids like to be cool. Kids may want a lot of stuff, but don't need it! Sometimes kids give you headaches, but that doesn't mean you should yell at them. You should be glad you have kids! Help them with their homework if they need it. They should also know their grades and where they are going.

Jason, age 10

Kids don't care if parents say no sometimes, but saying no all the time children get bad feelings. When a parent says yes more often than no, that gives kids confidence.

Nick, age 11

Artwork by Kacey, age 6

We're not angels. Kids can get messy so don't scream at them if they have mud on their clothes with some exceptions, so don't worry it comes out in the wash.

Melissa, age 9

Well, sometimes kids can be pretty selfish and bad. Some kids can be sneaky.

Emily, age 8

Parents should know that kids get confused very easily. We don't understand things as children did in their time. They should know we are hurt when parents speak to us in a harsh way. It makes us think that they don't love us anymore or they wanted a different child.

Lauren, age 10

I think they should know that we are justlike them and we have feelings too.

Erica, age 9

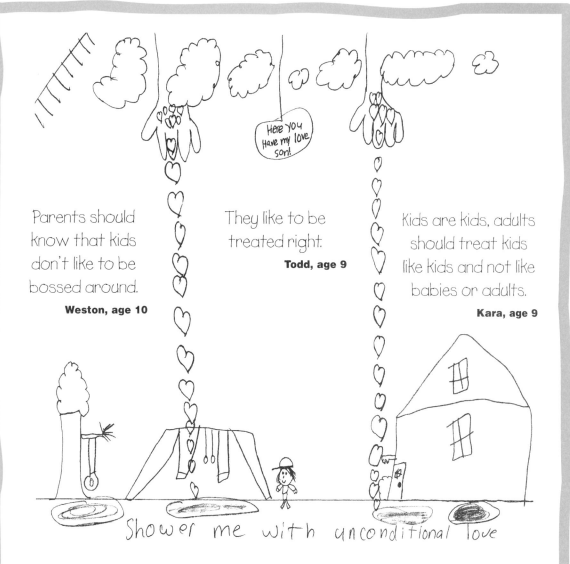

Parents should know that kids don't like to be bossed around.

Weston, age 10

They like to be treated right.

Todd, age 9

Kids are kids, adults should treat kids like kids and not like babies or adults.

Kara, age 9

Here you Have my love son!

Shower me with unconditional love

Artwork by Jonathon, age 8

What Would You Like to Learn From Your Parents?

What I would like to learn from my parents
is what it is like becoming a parent and
what is was like being a kid.

Emily, age 8

I would like to know what my parents think they have done wrong so I don't make those same mistakes.

Melissa, age 9

I want my dad to teach me how to fix things and to drive and to fly jets.

Tim, age 6

Artwork by Tim, age 6

I want to learn from my mom not to do drugs or smoke. I want to learn from my dad to tell the truth. My mom always tells me not to be so picky and like the things I have. My mom teaches me to be thankful for our family and love our family. She even wants me to love our dogs. They always teach me good things from bad. I even love them when they're mean, because I know they're only trying to show me the right stuff. I think they are nice. I really love my mom, dad and my sister, plus my two dogs. And my mom is pregnant and we're going to have a boy. I'm sure I'll love him too.

Danielle, age 8

I would like to learn how to run a family from my parents.

Weston, age 10

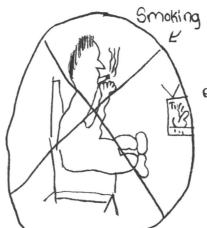

I would like to learn about the old days.

Todd, age 9

Artwork by Molly, age 10

I would like to learn how to run a family from my parents.

Weston, age 10

Hey Mom will you teach me to cross the road?

Thanks

Why sure honey

That's why i'm here

I want to know how to change a diaper. I bet it will stink. I want to learn how to wash the dishes and do the laundry.

Nick, age 6

I think it would be for my parents to teach me how to drive. If I never knew how to drive when I grow up I wouldn't be able to visit people in other cities. That would be dreadful!

Aaron, age 10

Artwork by Michael, age 9

I would like to learn how to get
a college scholarship and how to
make it to driver's education.

Brad, age 10

I would like to know what it is like to
be a parent from my parents.

Katie, age 10

I would like to ask my parents how to wash the dishes, to clean the house, how to keep my room clean, how to make my bed, how to help my brother be good instead of wild, to make friends and how to do math.

Kacey, age 6

I want to learn how to plant a seed. I want to learn how to do the dishes.

Aaron, age 7

The game of life. How to be responsible and independent.

Amber, age 11

I want to have my mom and dad kiss me and hug me every night. My mom and dad read to me every night. I want my mom to teach me to push a button on the washing machine.

Jennifer, age 7

How do you hire your kids to clean the house? How do you change the baby's diaper? How do you clean the dishes? How do you clean the toilet?

Kevin, age 6

I would like to learn from my parents what their childhood was like.

Steven, age 8

I would ask my parents how to fly a jet, how to drive a car, how to ride a whale.

John, age 6

Artwork by Amber, age 7

If You Were to Instruct Your Parents On How to Be Parents, What Would You Tell Them?

If I were to instruct my parents, I would tell them to be kind and understanding. I'll expect them to listen to all I say. That makes it easier for them and me. They should try to understand what we mean when we have a problem.

Lauren, age 10

I would tell them that being a parent is a very hard job because if you have a lot of kids, you have to pick up after them and wash all of their clothes and sheets.

Jason, age 9

Dear Mom and Dad,
    If you don't fight I would be happy but you are going to live apart. If you are nice to Dad, if you are nice to Mom, I would give you some money. If you are nice to me would you give me a yes or no?

Jason, age 7

I want every parent to love.

Liz, age 6

If I were to instruct my parents I would tell them to let kids watch movies past their bedtime and I would tell them to listen to kids and not move their bedrooms around without asking.

Michelle, age 10

Artwork by Liz, age 6

Hey parents listen, all my kids at school that have divorced parents are disappointed about it. It is hard for kids to deal with stuff like this especially the little ones. I know I have to go to my dad's every other weekend and at least once a day on the week days, well at least he wants me to. My dad loves me and I love him. We do things together just the two of us like camp out and dinner out. So if it is hard for you, try to show that you love your kid more.

Michelle, age 10

Artwork by Steven, age 8

If I were to instruct my parents on how to be parents, I would tell them to take care of me and bring me lunch every Friday.

Jessica, age 10

If I were to instruct my parents I would tell them to understand us when we have a problem. And to listen to what we have to say and not just ignore us and talk about something else. Parents should know that kids get confused sometimes on what they're saying. Parents should know what kids are learning in school.

Katie, age 10

What it takes to make a good parent is a loving person who cares for their children and a person who doesn't beat their children. If a parent has more than one child they need to do everything fairly and be nice to all of their children. If a parent treats them badly then the people who they treated bad will treat their kids bad because that's how they got treated when they were kids. If the parents want their kids to have a good life then they should care for them, be a loving person and be nice to them. I think that's what makes a good parent and that makes kids have a good life.

Cassie, age 10

I think an ideal parent would be a patient parent. If your kid doesn't understand something, explain it to them and if they still don't understand, don't yell. Compare it to something they understand and like, then explain it again. Here's another example, if you tell your kid to do something like a chore of some kind and they don't do it right away don't yell. Wait 15 minutes or so then go tell them again just to make sure they heard or didn't forget. Then if they still don't do it and you're sure they heard you, then tell them they can't watch TV for the rest of the night or something, but don't spank them or send them to bed without supper because that makes them believe that you don't like them. Don't yell at your kid for no reason and if you do and they start crying don't yell again, apologize. That's what I think an ideal parent would be.

Kim, age 11

Artwork by Joshua, age 6

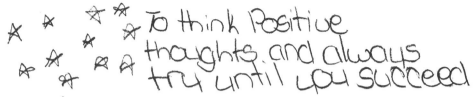

To think Positive thoughts, and always try until you succeed

Teach me to dream and reach for the stars.

Shouldn't Do: Parents shouldn't yell at kids so much. They shouldn't hit kids. Shouldn't leave kids alone in an empty house with a sitter or older person there (kids ages 10 and under). Shouldn't leave kids in a running car. Never let a little kid go out by the street. Don't spoil kids.

Should Do: Should reward kids for doing good things. Try to let kids do things that are good for kids to do. Try to teach kids to do things right. Let your kids be educated. Teach them as much as you can.

Help kids do the right thing by not doing the Shouldn'ts and by doing the Shoulds.

Erin, age 11

Artwork by Laura, age 9

What Do Parents Do That Makes You Mad?

My parents sometimes make me mad by yelling at me, making me clean up after my sister and making me clean up my room when my brother made the mess.

Aaron, age 10

They make me mad when they don't listen to me.

Cathy, age 8

Mom makes me mad when she embarrasses me in front of other people. Mom makes me mad when she treats me like a baby. I get mad when she makes me brush my teeth. I love my mom, but why does she have to make me mad?

Kristen, age 8

Artwork by Darrin, age 6

Parents make me mad when they embarrass me, make me feel low about myself and punish me for something I didn't do.

Amber, age 11

They make me go to bed when there is something good on TV. I hate when I come back from my friend's house and my parents ask me what I played there.

Dawn, age 10

My favorite show comes on at 8:30 which means it's on until 9:00 so I have to go to bed when it's over. So one day it's an hour special and your parent or parents won't let you stay up and watch it. That's what gets me mad. Or on Sundays they make you go to church. Sometimes people fall asleep in church.

Carin, age 11

Artwork by Sarah, age 7

My parents do four things that make me mad. One of them is when I'm watching TV they turn my show off and turn theirs on. When I'm playing with my friends and they say play with your sister too. My parents make me go to bed at 9:30, I want to go to bed at 10:00. And, they make me eat chop suey and I don't like it.

Melissa, age 8

My parents make me mad when I'm right and they say that they're right, but I'm really right and then we get into a big fight. Then they feel really bad and now we don't get in fights often.

Keri, age 8

Parents make me mad by yelling at me for not doing the right things. They should just tell us nicely.

Katie, age 10

My mom makes me mad because she doesn't buy me toys. My mom makes me happy because my mom pulls my tooth.

Bill, age 6

Artwork by Jacob, age 6

My mom makes me go to my room. My mom stays on the phone too long.

Jordan, age 6

I don't like it when I'm playing games and she says it is time to go to the store. Then I have to pick my game up. If I was the parent I would call the babysitter and let my child play.

Amanda, age 11

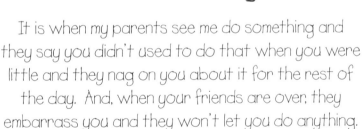

When my parents embarrass me in front of my friends.

Amanda, age 11

It is when my parents see me do something and they say you didn't used to do that when you were little and they nag on you about it for the rest of the day. And, when your friends are over, they embarrass you and they won't let you do anything.

Curlisha, age 10

The top 10 things that parents do that make you mad:

1. Make you go to bed at 8:00.
2. Make you take a nap.
3. Let your sister do something you can't.
4. Make you stay out of the mud in the yard.
5. Ground you for a month
6. Make you buy your own car.
7. Make you go to school on a half day.
8. Make you do your homework.
9. Don't let you play video games when you are the only one home.
10. Don't let you call your friend when you are home alone.

Cameron, age 8

My mom makes me sad and mad when she yells at me and makes me cry. I LOVE my mommy even though she sometimes makes me mad.

Andrew, age 7

Cleaning my room, vacuuming my floor and waking me up in the morning.

Stephen, age 7

What Does It Take to Be a Parent?

Show your love for your child or children. Do not abuse them! Show an equal amount of love to all of your children! Try to understand their reasoning and treat them how you would like to be treated! When they grow up and need privacy try to understand that. Do not yell at them a lot, it makes us think that you don't love us.

Bethany, age 9

What makes a good parent is how much the parent cares and loves the child. Not if they get a "Parent of the Year" award, it's the love and care that count.

Alissa, age 9

Artwork by Amber, age 6

I would tell them if you want to be a better parent to love, pay attention, spend time with them and teach them things.

Julie, age 9

Drinking Beer + Smoking

Inhaling fumes

A good parent helps you with your math. They take you out to eat. They buy you toys. They take care of you. They teach you not to take drugs, not to smoke and drink. They teach you how to clean. They teach you how to be calm when you're mad. But the most important thing is that they love you.

Wendy, age 8

Part of being a good parent is not doing drugs, but if you do drugs don't do them in front of your children if you don't want them to get in the habit. BY DOING DRUGS YOU CAN LOSE YOUR LIFE!

Tara, age 9

To be a good parent you have a
responsibility for life. You have to let
the child live their own life, but yet tell
them what's right and wrong.

Molly, age 10

I hate when parents fight. I think parents should solve problems in a calmer way. Children should learn responsibility and discipline. They should learn to share, read and to behave. Parents should be good to their kids. They should help you with whatever you need help with. A parent should be with you when you are sick. Be a good example for your children to follow. Teach them to stand up for themselves. That's what it takes to be a good parent.

Matthew, age 9

I'm going to tell you "WHAT IT TAKES TO BE A PARENT." I think it must be a big responsibility, probably the biggest. A parent must provide clothing, food, a warm place to live, discipline and lots of love. Parents also need to teach their children right from wrong. Being a parent isn't like a job that you go to work 9:00 to 5:00. When you are a parent you work all the time, at least that's what my mom says. Being a parent never stops because after your children are grown you will probably become a grandparent.

Megan, age 9

Artwork by Shawna, age 10

It takes a lot of love from kids always. Also a good husband or wife and that goes along with a well kept house. You need to have a good job that provides good money for things like food and clothes for your kids and yourself. You also have to be fun, give a little slack, but don't let kids take control over you. I think that's what it takes to be a parent.

Jessica, age 9

Our parents go to work so we can eat out and drink. They teach me not to smoke or drink so we don't grow up and have troubles with our body. They try to be the best they can. They try not to yell at us. If we didn't have parents we would be living on the streets or in cardboard boxes. I'm glad to have a parent.

Ryan, age 9

A good mom and dad should give kids a lot of love and maybe a pet or two.

Amber, age 6

Artwork by Jessica, age 9

What makes a good parent is not making your children make their beds, do laundry, wash dishes, and vacuum. Taking your child to his or her grandparent's house ought to make them happy. A parent could give their children a break from each other by sending one to a relative's house for a few weeks and the parents could keep the other one.

Michelle, age 11

Some parents can be too strict. They need to lighten up a little and let us grow up. They get too worried, sometimes I mean, it's just normal for them to worry, but at times they go overboard. Like if you stay at a friend's house a little bit longer they start calling all over the place saying have you seen her (him).

Carin, age 11

I would tell them that if there was a problem that they should listen to both sides of the story before punishment.

Amber, age 6

Artwork by Kelly, age 9

Artwork by Michelle, age 11

The
End

About the Author

Kari Cimbalik's work as a Sunday school teacher for 3- and 4-year-old children taught her the importance of listening to how children see the world. She is currently at work on her second book, *Spend Time with Me,* and is also writing a series of children's books. She lives in Auburn Hills, Michigan.